AMERICAN BIRTHRIGHTS

UNDERSTANDING "AMERICAN NATIONAL", <u>PRIVATE CITIZEN</u> BIRTH RIGHTS

Aran Alton Ardaiz

Truth of God Ministry
Hawaiian Islands

Published by
Truth of God Ministry
Hawaiian Islands

© Copyright 2009 by Aran Alton Ardaiz

Common law Copyright Aran Ardaiz, 2009

General Delivery, (Box 62107)
Manoa Station, Island of Oahu
The Hawaiian Islands
(U.S.P.Z. Exempt)

ISBN-10: 0-615-29734-X
ISBN-13: 978-0-615-297347-1

AMERICAN BIRTHRIGHTS

UNDERSTANDING "AMERICAN NATIONAL", PRIVATE CITIZEN BIRTH RIGHTS

**America! I love you!
Wake up! You are dying!**

SUBJECT: THE LAWFUL AND LEGAL JURISDICTIONAL DIFFERENCE AND USE BETWEEN THE ALL CAPITALIZED LEGAL FICTION AND THE PROPER ENGLISH LANGUAGE SPELLED BIRTH NAME.

Our State's birth, *"inalienable"*[1] "Private Citizen"[2] American birth rights, are preserved under the *"common-law"*[3] in our proper

---

1 **Inalienable rights.** Rights which are not capable of being surrendered or transferred without the consent of the one possessing such rights; e.g. freedom of speech or religion, due process, and equal protection of the laws. (Source: Black's Law Dict. 6th Ed. Page 759)

2 **Private.** Affecting or belonging to private individuals as distinct from public generally. Not official; not clothed with office. (Source: Blacks Law Dict. 6th Ed. Page 1195)

3 **Common law.** "...California Civil Code, Section 22.2, provides that the "common law of England, so far as it is not repugnant to or inconsistent with the constitution of the United States, or the Constitution or laws of this State, is the rule of decision in all the courts of this State." For complete definition, please go to the source in... (Source: Black's Law Dictionary, 6th Ed. Page 276)

1

English language spelled birth names... not in the ALL CAPITALIZED created fiction name owned and used by the Federal United States Government.

DIFFERENT NAMES FOR DIFFERENT JURISDICTIONS OF LAW AND CITIZENSHIP

HOW TO CAPTURE AMERICAN NATIONALS

There has been much misunderstood discussion and ignorance regarding the proper and / or lawful birth names versus the pseudonym *(fictitious)* ALL CAPITALIZED names. **To be more specific, a powerful difference exists between my lawful, natural birth name, "*Aran Alton: Ardaiz*", an American, State's born living soul, a "*National*"[4] and "Private Citizen"; and, the lesser, created, 14th Amendment all CAPITALIZED fiction name of the U.S. Government.** *(The use of the colon [:] after the given names, historically and by proper language usage, denotes "of the"*

---

4 National (Citizen). ...A person owing permanent allegiance to a state. 8 USCA§ 1101. The term "national" as used in the phrase "national of the United States" is broader than the term "citizen". Brassert v. Biddle. D.C.Conn., 59 F. Supp. 457, 462. (Source: Black's Law Dictionary, 6th Ed., Page 1024)

family or clan. Therefore the name would be interpreted and read as "Aran Alton" of the "Ardaiz" family or clan.)

My name spelled in the proper English-language <u>reveals that I am a *"Private Citizen"*</u> As an American <u>State's born</u> *Private Citizen (American National)* I am definitely not an immigrant, civil servant, public official, corporation, naturalized *"citizen"*, member of the military or corporate officer. **I have never abandoned nor with knowledge, signed away my sovereign State's birth rights to become a lesser in right Federal jurisdiction, created, fiction U.S. federalized public *"citizen"*.**

My birth name when spelled in upper and lower case letters, according to proper English language cursive and scripted usage, <u>reflects who I am</u>. <u>This spelling reflects a *"Private Citizen"* under my sovereign State's "common-law" with my birth rights and inalienable rights intact</u>. Most definitely I am not the partially CAPITALIZED, or all CAPITALIZED, named U.S. Federal *"citizen"* <u>without birth rights</u> under the *"Civil Rights Acts"* of the Federal jurisdiction.

STATE'S RIGHTS SOVEREIGNS

The term *"sovereign"*[5] is a title used by many Americans who do not know the origin or basis of that word. It is a title derived from natural birth, in one of the 48 *"contiguous"* States of the Union, with birth rights and inalienable rights intact. In contrast, **U.S. Federal "citizens" are not "sovereigns"**... they are created, fiction *"citizens"* without birth rights!

The American born National is a "sovereign", e.g. *A* ***"Private Citizen"*** *within the* <u>*American Union of States*</u> *and is one in whom is vested the right of sovereign power and authority over the government.* I repeat, that primary birth right is that of being born within one of the 48 *contiguous* States of the *American Union of States, a Republic.*

In America, every sovereign State is in affect, <u>an independent nation within our greater American National Union of States</u>, e.g. *"united"* States, a Republic.

If I had been born in Washington D.C. , or any

5 **Sovereign people.** The political body, consisting of the entire number of citizens and qualified electors, who in their collective capacity, possess the powers of sovereignty and exercise them through their chosen representatives. See Scott v. Sanford, 19 How. 404, 15 L.Ed. 691. (Source: Black's Law Dict. 6th Ed., Page 1,396)

of the military jurisdictions or federal IRS *"States" (e.g. territories like American Samoa, Guam, Puerto Rico, [Panama], American Virgin Islands or the acknowledged foreign soil of the Hawaiian Islands),* I would be a U.S. Federal *"public citizen",* better described as an *"artificial person"* under Article 1 Section 8 jurisdiction *(e.g. as a public servant, civil service, military and corporate side).*

While in that jurisdiction, I would be a foreigner to the *American Constitution of the Republic* due to the simple lack of a sovereign State's birth right. **This differentiation is affirmed by the simple convoluted spelling of my birth name.**

CITIZENSHIP IS VOLUNTARY

"While we blindly slumbered in our wealth
and great gains, our justice systems, which
we have ignored, have become tyrannical
and we shall soon loose both our gains and
our freedoms to tyrants in power."

- Author.

WHERE DID THE ALL CAPITALIZED FICTION NAME COME FROM?

I most definitely am not the legal fiction, created *"corporate person,"* titled and improperly printed as **"ARAN ALTON ARDAIZ"** or **"Aran Alton ARDAIZ"**. The printed, convoluted spelling of my name reflects a distinctive, grammatically abusive modification of my birth name. It is a pseudonym or alias created for America's *Emancipated Slaves* under the *(1868)* 14th Amendment of the American Constitution to provide *Emancipated Slaves* a distinctively different, yet lesser, U.S. *"Federal"* citizenship without State's birth rights.

The U.S. Congress owns that fictitious creation which it unlawfully implements. **It reflects a foreign citizenship without birth rights, state's rights or inalienable rights.** Primarily, as presently utilized against American *"Nationals"*, it erases one's inalienable birth rights and State's rights by changing the jurisdiction of law and the lawful **American Republic 48 Star Flag** that you thought you were submitted to, to the fifty star military flag that is foreign to that birth right. As you can now see, there are two (2) types of citizenship in America and have been since the American Civil War; with two flags representing two very distinctly different jurisdictions of law.

THE PROPERLY SPELLED BIRTH NAME

The proper and lawful name given me as a child by my parents, when born in Monterey, *"California Republic"*, U.S.A., is, *"Aran Alton Ardaiz"*. I was born in the *"California Republic"*, a *"**sovereign State**"*[6] of the *American Union of States*, <u>and not in the lesser</u> *U.S. Federal jurisdiction* of the "corporate" Article 1, Section 8, de facto STATE OF CALIFORNIA. Yep, there are also two States, the sovereign one and the fiction or federalized one. The de facto federalized STATE OF CALIFORNIA *(utilizing the created, printed ALL CAPITALIZED NAME)* is not the sovereign *California Republic*. It is the imposter, de facto corporate STATE created by the Federal Government for U.S. Federal fiction *"public citizens"*, not American *"Nationals"* of

---

6 **Sovereign state.** States whose subjects or citizens are in the habit of obedience to them, and which are not themselves subject to any other (or paramount) state in any respect. The state is said to be semi-sovereign only, and not sovereign, when in any respect or respects it is liable to be controlled by a paramount government... (Black's Law Dict. 6th Ed. Page 1396)

the Republic and its Union of States. I am, by virtue of my *"natural"*[7] birth in the *California Republic* protected by the *"common-law"* of the sovereign California Republic Constitution as an *"American National"* and *"Private Citizen"*. Natural born citizens are *"Persons who are born within the jurisdiction of a national government, i.e., in its territorial limits, or those born of citizens temporarily residing abroad."*

As an American National, I have never, with knowledge, relinquished my *"natural"* State's birth rights. I am not a U.S. second-class, immigration status, <u>federal</u> U.S. *"public citizen"* under Article 1 Section 8 of that very same American Constitution <u>just because some lesser civil official or entity says I am.</u>

A *"public citizen"* or U.S. *"person"* is one who is a U.S. Federal *"citizen"* under the *U.S. Civil Rights Acts (legislated and statutory law)* and Article 1 Sec. 8 of the Constitution of the American Republic. If I was a *"public citizen"*, I would be <u>without sovereign State birth rights or full constitutional rights</u> and protection under the *American Constitution of the Republic*. A *"public citizen"* or *"citizen"* is an

---

7   **Natural born citizen.** (Source: Black's Law Dict. 6th Ed. Page 1026)

9

"Emancipated Slave", naturalized immigrant, civil servant, public official, member of the military or corporate officer. I have never knowingly or with knowledge abandoned or contracted away either my sovereign State birth rights or my *American National Private Citizenship.* Have you?

As an American *"Private Citizen"* born to a sovereign State titled the *California Republic*, one of the 48 *"contiguous"* States of the Union, I am automatically an *"American National Private Citizen"* under the *"common-law"* of my sovereign State Constitution and the **American Constitution of the *"Republic"*[8]** and its **Bill of Rights**. This provides me with a type of "dual" Citizenship of which one is a *"sovereign, State's right Citizenship"* by virtue of my birth within one of the 48 *contiguous* States of the Union.

AMERICA'S BASIC COMMON-LAW

The *"common-law"* *(as distinguished from statutory law which is created by the enactment of legislatures)* comprises the body of those principles and rules of action, relating to the

---

8 **Republican Government.** "A government in the republican form; a government of the people; a government by representatives chosen by the people." (Black's Law Dictionary, 6th Ed., Page 1303)

government and security of persons and property, which derive their authority solely from usages and customs of immemorial antiquity, or from the judgments and decrees of the courts recognizing, affirming and enforcing such usages and customs; and, in this sense, particularly the ancient unwritten law of England. <u>In general, it is a body of law that develops and derives through judicial decisions</u>, as distinguished from legislative enactments.

The *"common law"* is all the statutory and case law background of England and the American colonies *(since)* before the American Revolution. ... It consists of those principles, usage and rules of actions applicable to government and security of persons and property which do not rest for their authority upon any express and positive declaration of the will of the legislature.

When I served in the United States Military *(To protect the American People who lived under the Constitutions of the several States, e.g. Union of States)*, my name was deliberately changed into the printed ALL CAPITALIZED LETTERS to formally identify me as being outside of the American Constitution *(as a federally contracted military man with limited rights)* temporarily forfeiting my sovereign, constitutional, State's birth rights by simply submitting <u>by contract</u> to federal military jurisdiction and rule. By making this more personal, I hope to help you better understand just what's happened to our *"Private Citizen"* birth rights, freedoms and liberties.

Politicians, bankers, attorneys and judges have been for years trying to remove us from the common-law of our respective individual states, <u>which protects our birth rights and freedoms</u> *<u>(e.g. sovereign, inalienable rights)</u>* to move us into their federal legislated and statutory created law jurisdiction in <u>order to control us as their fiction *"citizens"*</u>. To totally remove us from our sovereign State's birth rights, they have created the Uniform Commercial Code (U.C.C.) which is designed to replace our greater, rightful, primary "common-law".

MY INALIENABLE RIGHTS

The grammatically proper English language spelling, of my birth name is: *"Aran Alton: Ardaiz"*. <u>That name, when scripted</u> *(written out in cursive)* is my lawful *"<u>seal</u>"*. It grants

---

9 Seal. An impression upon wax, wafer, or some other tenacious substance capable of being impressed. In current practice, a particular sign (e.g. L.S. [Lawful Signature].) or the word "seal" is made in lieu

12

or denies authority to others; it obligates or denies rights in contract format. It is my seal as an *American National Private Citizen* affirming my authority under the *Constitution of the American Republic* and is based upon my natural birth within one of the forty-eight (48) *contiguous (united) States of our American Union.*

My *"inalienable"*[10] American Constitutional and State Rights are protected and preserved in my properly English language spelled birth name! As an American National, my inalienable rights are my rights which are not capable of being surrendered or transferred without my *(explicit)* consent being the one possessing such rights; e.g., freedom of speech or religion, due process, and equal protection of the laws; the common-law right to a jury of my peers; right to travel, to bear arms; right of habeas corpus; not to be deprived of life, liberty or property, without due process of law; freedom from false arrest; right to speedy trial, ect. No one can take those rights from me, but I can reject them, abandon them, or forfeit them with or without my explicit consent. It

---

of an actual seal to attest the execution of the instrument. .. (Black's Law Dict. 6th Ed. Page 1348)

10 **Inalienable rights.** (Source: Black's Law Dict. 6th Ed. Page 759)

is called contracting away my rights.

The right to contract my rights away is preserved under *Article 1 Section 10 of the American Constitution (Right to contract)*. Unfortunately, this Article of the American Constitution has been deviously used by the U.S. Federal Government *(a lesser, Article 1 Section 8, U.S. Constitutional jurisdiction of law and right)* to take *American National Private Citizens (e.g. sovereigns)* out from under their natural birth names, State birth rights and <u>48 Star American National Flag</u> in order to place them through their ignorance into that lesser federal jurisdiction within Article 1 Section 8 *(a jurisdiction foreign to their birth)* under a foreign, <u>50 star military flag</u> *(e.g. as "public ̲citizens" of Washington D.C.)*.

(Excerpt from:)

The DECLARATION OF INDEPENDENCE

Declaration of the thirteen united States of America (July 4, 1776)

(The following is from the Preamble)

"...We hold these truths to be self-evident, that all men are created equal, that they are endowed by their Creator with certain unalienable Rights, that among these are Life, Liberty and the pursuit of Happiness. That to secure these rights, Governments are instituted among Men, <u>deriving their just powers from the consent of the governed</u>..." (Underlined emphasis by Author)

<u>INTERESTING POINT:</u>
Think this through.

It appears to this Author, that only the U.S. Federal *(military / foreign affairs)* jurisdiction is deep, deep in debt to the privately owned Federal Reserve Bank *(private bankers, et al)*.

State's born American Nationals <u>are not liable for income taxes</u> while under their sovereign State's birth right common-law jurisdiction and under their properly printed birth name seal *(signature)*, wherein their sovereign, inalienable rights exist (remember the 16th Amendment that didn't pass?).

Nationals only become liable if they *(are defrauded)* accept and submit to the use of the <u>created</u>, fiction name *(as "Taxpayers")* within the foreign, corrupted, <u>lesser constitutional</u> U.S. Federal jurisdiction, *e.g. abandon their rightful 48 Star Flag of the Republic, their respective birth State Flag and proper English language spelled birth name.*

CITIZENSHIP IS VOLUNTARY

TWO FLAGS – ONE IS FOREIGN!
OUR FLAG OF THE
AMERICAN REPUBLIC

Each flag represents a distinct jurisdiction.

The primary constitutional jurisdiction is that of the *American Flag of the Republic* and our *Union of States* which is still 48 Stars as lawfully affirmed under the "*Positive law*" of Title 4, Section 1 of the United States Code. I now quote that still active law:

"Section 1. Flag; stripes and stars on *The flag of the United States shall be thirteen horizontal stripes, alternate red and white; and the union of the flag shall be forty-eight stars, white in a blue field. (July 30, 1947, ch 389, 61 Stat. 642.)* **Interpretive Notes and Decisions:** *Placing a fringe on national flag, dimensions of flag, and arrangement of stars in union are matters of detail controlled by statute, but are within the discretion of President as Commander-In-Chief of Army and Navy. (1925) 34 Op Atty Gen 483)* (Underlining emphasis by Author)

The word "*shall*" in reference to the number of Stars in the union means "*must be*".

Nowhere can I find where the President, even as the Commander-In-Chief of the military, possesses lawful authority to add stars to our National Flag of the Republic. He can only <u>*"arrange"* them as evidenced above</u>.

HOW DID WE GET A
50 STAR FLAG?
IS IT REALLY A MILITARY FLAG?

<u>The other *(a constitutionally limited)* juris-diction</u> is represented by the *50 star federal government "flag"*[11] which <u>was unlawfully created</u> as a *"**military flag**"*[12] along with the Yellow Fringe *(by supposedly, but not really, adding two [2] stars to the 48 Star American Flag of the Republic)*. The new foreign flag was <u>unlawfully</u> and deliberately created by the unilateral action *(with only the lesser Federal*

---

11 **Law of the Flag.** In maritime law, the law of that nation or country whose flag is flown by a particular vessel. A ship owner who sends his vessel into a foreign port gives notice by his flag to all who enter into contracts with the master that he intends the law of that flag to regulate such contracts, and that they must either submit to its operation or not contract with him. (Source: Black's Law Dictionary, 6th Edition, Page 638.) AUTHOR'S NOTE: THIS ALSO OF COURSE APPLIES TO ANY PLACE WHERE THAT PARTICULAR FLAG FLIES, EVEN IN A COURT ROOM OR ON A DEFINED PARCEL OF LAND SO DESIGNATED, OR CLAIMED AS BEING UNDER THAT SPECIFIC AUTHORITY AND JURISDICTION, EVEN THOUGH TEMPORARILY SO.

12 **Military flag.** 1925 United States Attorney General Opinion No. 34, regarding military flag use. (4 USC 1, (1925 footnote) 34 Op Atty Gen 483. Also affirmed in 4 USCA Sections 1 and 2.

[military] Congressional approval) by then Commander-in-Chief, Dwight Eisenhower and not with the approval of the *National Congress of the Republic* as required by the American Constitution and *"Positive law" (by functioning outside of Positive law)*. The Commander-in-Chief of the United States Military under **Executive Order No. 10834** on **8-25-59**, <u>**created a brand new foreign flag;**</u> a new *50 star flag solely <u>for the federal, military jurisdiction</u>*.

The 50 star flag, because of its unlawful creation, is in fact, a *military flag*, with or without a yellow fringe on its perimeter.

With or without the yellow fringe, the *fifty-star flag* is still a military flag. Please note that this *fifty-star military flag* flies in the courtrooms of the Article 1 *(lesser)* federal courts <u>which courts are not the required Article III, Constitutional Courts of the</u> *<u>American Republic and our Union of States</u>* as set forth and required by the *American Constitution of the Republic*.

The unlawful new flag is a <u>lesser in right flag</u> which represents only the <u>constitutionally limited, Article 1 Section 8,</u> federal

jurisdiction, in contrast to our 48 Star Flag of the Republic which represents our lawful 48 sovereign States of the Union AND the federal jurisdiction as well.

If yellow fringe is placed around the perimeter of our Forty-Eight Star Flag of the Republic, it also becomes a military flag. <u>The yellow fringe mutilates *(makes unlawful)* the flag</u> as affirmed by **Title 4 USC Section 3** by either attachment of fringe, adding a third color, or both.

<u>Abusing flag law</u>: The U.S. federal jurisdiction intrudes into the sovereign State's rights national jurisdiction *(as if it is an ocean of nations)* <u>to serve flag notice</u> of its contracting rights *(as if into a foreign "sea port", so to speak)*.

Therefore, *American National <u>Private Citizens</u>* MUST, <u>with knowledge</u>, function under their *Positive law Title 4 United States Code, Section 1 Flag* (4 USC 1) of the American Republic! There is no *Positive law* that overrules this American <u>Private Citizen</u> right, truth and fact of law.

My American Flag is the *Positive law*, Forty-Eight (48) Star National Flag of the American

Republic and its Union of States! Which flag is yours?

CITIZENSHIP IS VOLUNTARY

"...That this nation, under God, shall have
a new birth of freedom..."

- Abraham Lincoln

UNDERSTANDING "AMERICAN NATIONAL", PRIVATE

CITIZENSHIP BIRTH RIGHTS

BACK TO THAT NAME
THING CREATED FOR
"EMANCIPATED SLAVES"

The improper type of English language pseudonym or alias name was created in order to distinguish the *"Emancipated Slave" (a created federal "public citizen")* from the Caucasian *"American National Private Citizen" (or "sovereign")*. The *"Emancipated Slave"* was a supposedly freed slave as was designated under the *"Emancipation Proclamation"* of Abraham Lincoln issued on January 1, 1863, declaring that all persons held in slavery in certain designated states and districts were and should remain free.

THE "NEW 1869 SLAVE ACT"
DO SLAVES HAVE BIRTHRIGHTS?

No! Slaves did not then nor do they now possess any type of birth right citizenship... they are possessions, e.g. "things", hence the 14th Amendment Congress creation of the federal *"public citizen"*. Do you have birth rights? Are you a slave? <u>By what printed name</u> do you identify yourself? This new federal fiction type, created *"public citizen"* does not possess Constitutional rights *(State*

23

or Federal), State's birth rights or inalienable rights and freedoms. It is far inferior to the *"Private Citizen"* birth right possessed by the then *(1868),* biased, in power, *"Caucasian" American Nationals* of Congress.

The true *American National* is a *"sovereign",* domiciled under his proper English language spelled birth name and America's 48 Star National Flag. The *American National* gained that "sovereign" right by being born to one of the 48 *"contiguous"* sovereign *States of the Union.*

Because the federal fiction *"citizen", "person" or "thing"* was created by the United States Government; it *(e.g. the name and the person it is attached to)* are in fact, owned or possessed *(enslaved?)* by the United States Federal Government! It is the government's name and *"person"* to legally own by creation, **"custom and usage"**[13].

---

13 Custom and (common) usage. Definition - U.C.C. § 1-205[2]: "A usage or practice of the people, which, by common adoption and acquiescence, and by long and unvarying habit, has become compulsory, and has acquired the force of law with respect to the place or subject-matter to which it relates. It results from a long series of actions, constantly repeated, which have, by such repetition and by uninterrupted acquiescence, acquired the force of a tacit and common consent. A parole evidence rule does not bar evidence of custom or usage to explain or supplement a contract or memorandum of the parties." (Author's Note: The UCC is used to replace our sovereign State "common law" where

Since World War II and before, truth and distinction between types of citizenship has been cautiously and deliberately removed from our textbooks in our grammar schools, high schools and colleges. Therefore, how can you be expected to make intelligent decisions when the facts requiring that knowledge of citizenship and rights have been deliberately hidden from you? You cannot! You're ignorant not because you do not have the mental capability to comprehend and make intelligent decisions, but because you have been denied the very truth and knowledge necessary upon which to make those intelligent and competent decisions. This deliberately designed, programmed action to deceive is corruption by our extremely political justice system and those political public civil servants we have elected and hired to serve and protect us.

MY IDENTITY

The lawful, proper spelling in the English language of the birth name given me by my parents at my birth **is my lawful identity**.

As a child, until the age of consent or age permitted for lawful contract, <u>no one has the</u>

our birth rights and inalienable rights are preserved.)

25

authority to modify or change your birth name without your explicit consent. Again, this is your identity…this is who you are! It is very, very personal. It tells all others in the world that you are lawfully distinct from all of them. If changed without your consent due to your ignorance that that change creates, that becomes an unlawful act of fraud against you. If done in an organized, programmed and deliberate manner to achieve an unlawful affect or advantage over you, a living soul *(a "living soul" or "human being" as differentiated from the created "thing", or "fictitious person")*, that becomes what is known under law as, *"__constructive fraud__"*[14], a criminal offense. **It is identity theft on a massive scale exercised by government fraud and corruption. It is the stealing of your birthright, birth name, State's rights and God given inalienable rights *(freedoms)*!** All this corruption is being done with the fullness of knowledge by our lying elected politicians, our very liberal, political, compromising of justice, judiciaries and money focused professional legalists, all lacking integrity!

---

14 Constructive fraud. Exists where conduct, though not actually fraudulent, has all actual consequences and all legal effects of actual fraud…. Breach of legal or equitable duty which, irrespective of moral guilt, is declared by law to be fraudulent because of its tendency to deceive others or violate confidence. (Source: Black's Law Dict. 6th Ed., Page 314)

What I believe is so wonderfully unique about your proper, lawful birth name is that it provides you with lawfully protected <u>inalienable</u>, God given birth rights and liberties that even attorneys and judges cannot strip away!

Birth rights are determined by the following:

a) Natural heritage *(Citizenship)* of my parents.

b) The land of my birth *(Nation)*

c) State or Province within that Nation as pertaining to *"dual"* citizenship *(State and National Citizenship)*.

d) The proper grammatical spelling of my birth name which provides and guarantees me my inalienable rights.

FACT: The American Flag of Forty-Eight Stars is still <u>the living</u> *Positive law* Flag of the American Republic and our Union of States, as <u>affirmed under Title 4 USC Section 1</u>.

"The people are the masters
of both Congress and courts, not to
overthrow the Constitution, but to
overthrow the men who pervert it!"

- Abraham Lincoln

CONTRACTING AWAY
YOUR CHILD'S AND YOUR
OWN BIRTH RIGHTS

A living soul *(a human being)*, under the laws of his land *(State)*, cannot lawfully change his or her birth name until the age permitted by law for lawful right to contract *(within that sovereign State of birth)*. That age has been lowered in most states from twenty-one (21) to eighteen (18) years. Therefore, any change to the lawful birth name by convoluted spelling *(or changes of any kind)* is not lawful if done prior to that lawful age of the right to contract. This is an important point. – DON'T FORGET THIS FACT OF LAWFUL RIGHT.

In today's society, children *(not "kids": kids = goats)* are not taught the basics of grammar, the importance of their birth names or the importance of their citizenship rights under Almighty God.

In what is most often a misunderstood usage of the name *"American"*, most people walk with the presumption that they are in fact, *"American National Private Citizens"*. If you as a parent have given away your child's birth name legally *(but not lawfully)*, and assumed the fiction ALL CAPITALIZED NAME identity, you have in fact given away their *American National* and *Private Citizenship* status *(as well as their sovereign and inalienable rights)* e.g. State's birth rights.

WHAT ABOUT MY BIRTH RIGHTS?

What did I just say? I said, you may call yourself an *"American Citizen" (e.g. "National")* but IF you have permitted your name to be changed *(Either with or without your written consent)* to the printed ALL CAPITALIZED PSEUDONYM *(fictitious name),* you are not an *"American National Private Citizen"*. You have become a lesser federal, second-class, *"United States immigration status citizen"* <u>foreign to your State's birth rights</u> and protective State "common law" rights that give you your inalienable sovereignty under both State and National Constitutions!

WHAT'S YOUR IDENTITY?

As stated, if you identify yourself as a 14th Amendment, federal *"thing"* or *"public citizen"* outside of your birth jurisdiction, you no longer possess your *"inalienable sovereign rights"*; you have only <u>legislated</u>, <u>statutory</u>

"Civil Rights", just like the freed black slaves after and since the Civil War. If you changed jurisdictions, you will have lowered and abandoned your *(greater birth right standard of)* National citizenship!

So, have you given away your birth rights? Are you now under Article 1, Sections 8 and 10, of the American Constitution, which is the federal, military flag jurisdiction of law foreign to that of your sovereign State's *"common-law"*? That U.S. federal jurisdiction *(military)* is supposed to protect the *American National Private Citizen* e.g. sovereign *(one under his lawful, English language spelled birth name)*, against America's foreign enemies.

THE MILITARY NAME

When discharged from the military, we were released from active duty military service under the contracted, printed ALL CAPITALIZED name to return to our sovereign birth State where our birth rights are protected under the varied *"common-law"* of that particular State. Since you left the U.S. Military did you recapture your birth name wherein your inalienable rights as an *American National* and *Private Citizen* are preserved? Think!

31

BIBLICAL BIRTHRIGHT TRANSFER

In the **Holy Scriptures, Genesis 25: 30-34,** *"Esau despised his birth right"* because he didn't see any immediate *"profit"*. The benefit to him was far away and he saw it as a responsibility not worth the contract *(Covenant)* God had ordained. Under the Law of God, all of his father's *(Isaac's)* assets would be his, as would the responsibilities of his mother and the minor children, if any. Responsibility is something Esau didn't want or he would have valued his birth right, which was his being the first born, by law and custom.

Why have we neglected our rights and birth right citizenship? How did we get where we are? Are we staying there? Really, it all depends on how we see and value our birth rights, our freedoms, liberties and citizenship.

WHERE IS YOUR SECURITY?

Question: Is your security in the many false and inflated government promises and an uncertain promised future financial security or in the National birthrights given us by Almighty God?

Devious, misguided people in *"corporate"* state judiciaries and *"corporate"* state governments *(our civil service servants)* operating within the statutory jurisdiction of the Federal United States *(the Article 1 Sections 8 and 10, 50 Star military jurisdiction)* modify and change the names of *American Nationals* at birth for a reason. They can today create more blind tax paying *"non-persons" (e.g. "citizens" "corporations", and other "things" which are tax liable fictions).*

THEY CREATE FICTION CITIZENS

Governments cannot create human life. They can only create fictions like legal persons without birth rights, corporations, corporate persons etc. I qualify a *"non-person"* as one of these.

Our government civil servants, following orders from above convert our *American National Private Citizens,* who have been kept ignorant, into lesser *"Second Class, immigration status "federal, corporate, legal fiction citizens"* in order to remove them from their inalienable rights inherent by sovereign State's birth so as to burden them. This conversion is accomplished by simply utilizing the fiction name that sounds the same, but is not. This newly applied *"legal fiction"* name is then identified with the *"living soul"* or natural man who fails to distinguish the difference. Your signature *(seal)* on a document with the printed fiction, partial or ALL CAPITALIZED name gives/ grants your acknowledgement and approval by the formal endorsement of the fiction name, as being your own.

SCRIPTING THE ALL CAP NAME

Such an improper spelling of one's name is not a proper use of the English language, which is a scripted language, as mentioned previously. The proof of that fact is that it cannot be written *(scripted, written in cursive)*. You cannot script or write a name created in the printed ALL CAPITALIZED format only because the capitalized letters begin with a short down stroke or a short upstroke and when tied together will go up and down on a page and not in a straight line, which is not proper English cursive writing. It therefore serves as an alias, unlawfully utilized. It is also called a *"nom de guerre"*, or, *"name of war"*, having come to use off of tombstones… that of a dead man.

This improper, unlawful renaming of the *American National Private Citizen, "a living soul"* or natural man without his or her fullness of awareness, knowledge and explicit consent, as to the consequences, is fraud! The <u>lesser</u> federal government cannot lawfully convert you, a *"sovereign"* and *"living soul"* into a *"fiction"* or *"thing"* in order to manipulate you as their own <u>without your fullness of knowledge and agreement</u>, **e.g.** *"**consent**"*[15] *(a concurrence of the wills)*. They deceive you out of your ignorance and blind trust in their corrupted federal system.

The Federal United States Government and Court system *(lesser jurisdiction Article 1 Courts)* do not have lawful authority over the *American National, a Private Citizen (living soul and natural man)*, <u>*unless yielded,*</u> who functions lawfully under his proper birth name, his sovereign State's birth rights, his 48 Star National Flag and the flag of his rightful *"common-law"* State jurisdiction. These courts are limited to Washington D.C. and the federal territories defined by law, <u>not within</u> the jurisdiction of the sovereign States of the

---

15 **Consensual contract.** A term derived from the civil law, denoting a contract founded upon and completed by the mere consent of the contracting parties, without any external formality or symbolic act to fix the obligation. (Source: Black's Law Dict. 6th Ed. Page 304)

Union, or over sovereigns.

NOTICE: If you subject your proper, natural birth name citizenship to a foreign flag jurisdiction of law, you loose your rights by acquiescence and become subject to the laws of that foreign country or jurisdiction. This is your choice and your right! Remember, the federal government functions only under the created *"legal fiction"* name because they only have lawful authority over the *"thing"* and corporations that they create and own.... not you!

For you to stand for your birth rights and inalienable rights is not rebellion, nor is it treason, it is righteousness! <u>Righteousness is of Almighty God!</u>

Your birth right is God ordained, and as an *American National, Private Citizen,* and sovereign, no one has authority to take those rights from you! This right is based upon your having been born within one of the 48 *contiguous, sovereign* States of the ***American Union of States,*** and the respective *"common-law"* protection provided you by your birth State.

(Excerpt from our Constitution)

OUR TENTH AMENDMENT

The Tenth Amendment to our Constitution, known as **ARTICLE X** of The **BILL OF RIGHTS,** is still alive and working for us. I now quote it:

"The powers not delegated to the United States by the Constitution, nor prohibited by it to the States, are reserved to the States respectively, or to the people." (Underline emphasis by Author)

Very simply, we, "The People..." have failed to realize and recognize that we have allowed our individual, personal, State's birth right sovereign citizenship to be subordinated. As a supposedly free People, we have been asleep! We have allowed incompetent educators, paid off politicians and greedy, power seeking bankers to lull us with benefits to capture us in slumber.

"An unconstitutional act (or actions) is not law; it confers no rights; it imposes no duties; affords no protection; it creates no office; it is in legal contemplation, as inoperative as though it had never been passed."

- Norton vs. Shelby County, 118 US 425 p. 442.

THE GOVERNMENT CREATED FICTION "PERSON" UNDER THE FIFTY STAR FLAG

Fact: The U.S. Government created fiction *"person"*[16] is a federal *"citizen"* of Washington D.C., its territories, military and created corporate entities.

Let me define *"Person"* from the original First and Second Editions of Black's Law Dictionaries. The later editions, including the 6th Edition of Black's Law Dictionary cloud the real meaning of *"person"*.

(Black's First Edition) *Person.* *"A man considered according to the rank he holds in society, with all the rights to which the place he holds entitles him, and the duties which it imposes. 1 Bouv. Inst. No. 137. A human being considered as capable of having rights and being charged with duties; while a "thing" is the object over which rights may be exercised. Persons are divided by law into natural and*

---

16 **Person.** In general usage, a human being (i.e. natural person), though by statute term may include labor organizations, partnerships, associations, corporations, legal representatives, trustees, trustees in bankruptcy, or receivers... (Source: Black's Law Dict. 6th Ed., Page 1142.) Author's Clarifying Note: Under the common-law, you are a "natural 'person" or living human being. Under the civil law, you are a U.S. Federal "corporate person", "citizen", and corporation etc., not a living human being, a fiction.

39

artificial. Natural persons are such as the God of nature formed us; artificial are such as are created and devised by human laws, for the purposes of society and government, which are called "corporations" or "bodies politic." 1 Bl. Comm. 123."

(Black's Second Edition) Same as above definition but more so clarifies *"Person"* as:

*- **Artificial persons.** Such as are created and devised by law for the purposes of society and government, called "corporations" or "bodies politic." - **Natural persons.** Such as are formed by nature, as distinguished from artificial persons, or corporations. -**Private person.** An individual who is not the incumbent of an office."*

Therefore, government created fiction *"persons"* are distinctly different in rights at law from the living soul *(living natural person, e.g. "human being")* American National Private Citizen and sovereign. The American sovereign is superior in law and citizenship to that of the federal *"corporate legal fiction created" "person"* possessing the printed ALL CAPITALIZED fictitious name. Remember, the *"legal fiction name"* is that of second-class, immigration status United States *"federal fiction persons, citizens or things"* and is used to legally separate you from the American Constitution and your inalienable State's birth rights.

As mentioned, this *"legal fiction citizen"* is not under the *Positive law, 48 Star Flag of the American Republic*, but under the lesser jurisdiction *Federal United States 50 star military flag.*

CITIZENSHIP IS VOLUNTARY!

"Where the people fear the government you have tyranny; where the government fears the people, you have liberty."

- Thomas Jefferson

A POLICE STATE?
ABUSE OF POWER?

Most American sovereign State's born Nationals today have become lesser federal United States *"corporate created fiction citizens"* without their knowledge and awareness. Many are probably content to be so, many are not... but again, don't forget, **CITIZENSHIP IS VOLUNTARY. If not, we are all prisoners of a very corrupt *"police state"*[17] known as The U.S. Federal [military] Government** e.g. **without State birth rights or inalienable rights.** A police state condition exists when police power entrusted to government is abusive and exercised to excess, in violation of the inalienable Constitutional rights *(State and National)* of the American State's born *"National" "Private Citizen"* whose inalienable rights are presently infringed upon and denied... The taking away of a sovereign, Private Citizen's State's birth rights *(e.g. inalienable rights)* by a deliberate, corrupt and deceptive government practice such as presently implemented by the very corrupted U.S. Federal Government... *i.e.*

17 **Police state.** A nation in which the police, esp. a secret police, summarily suppresses any social, economic or political act that conflicts with governmental policy. (Source: Webster's Encyclopedic Unabridged Dictionary, 2001 Ed.)

the denial of the right to vote, and worship Almighty God etc., are good, present examples of abusive police power actions exercised by present blind state and federal government politicians and their judiciaries, that are ignorant of America's history.

<u>Based upon U.S. Federal Government fraud, you have lawful right to peacefully separate yourself from that subordinate, federalized, military jurisdiction</u>, just as you can be and/or get discharged from the U.S. Military. **You have that primary power, authority and right already vested in you *(as a sovereign)*. You can cancel the relationship *(contract)* and return to your sovereign State's right birth name and inalienable rights;** leaving the unauthorized federal corruption of your name and deprivation of your private and in-alienable rights behind you.

Your birth name, your citizenship and <u>inalienable</u> God Given Birth Rights are invaluable and beyond the comprehension, understanding, knowledge and education of most individuals today.

In the U.S. Federal jurisdiction as a fiction *"<u>c</u>itizen"*, you *(the submissive, waived rights*

National Private Citizen) are bound by contracts, statutory legislation and licensing as authorized under *Article 1 Sections 8 and 10 of the U.S. Constitution.* In their federal jurisdiction you are in *Admiralty* and *Equity* courts and you are not under your sovereign State birth right *"common-law"* or in constitutional Article III Courts where your inalienable rights *(like freedom of speech, religion, due process, equal protection under the law, the right to, travel, a common-law jury of 12 Peers, etc., etc.)* are preserved. **These Rights have been unlawfully removed along with your natural birth name!**

As mentioned, the present corporate STATE courts are U.S. federalized courts as well, and are under the lesser Article 1 *(U.S. Constitutional)* court jurisdiction. It appears to me that our foolish, un-American, elected state and federal politicians, as well as our very political, weak, liberal minded judges and greedy bankers have deliberately modified our court systems and removed our rights for their benefit and gain, at the expense of our State's born *"National"* inalienable freedoms and rights to justice.

Americans! The choice of citizenship is yours

and yours alone. Yes, you still do have choice.

Remember, only *Emancipated Slaves* were given this <u>lesser</u>; secondary government created fiction ***"public citizenship"***[18] without state's birth rights for a prejudicial reason and became the first wave of United States *"federal citizens"*. We American Nationals are presently the second wave.

Our corrupted U.S. Federal jurisdiction with its corrupted judges, bankers and politicians all know what they are doing. Do you?

---

18 Public Office. The right, authority, and duty created and conferred by law, by which for a given period, either fixed or by law or enduring the pleasure of the creating power, an individual is invested with some portion of the sovereign functions of government for the benefit of the public. An agency for the state, the duties of which involve in their performance the exercise of some portion of the sovereign power, either great of small. (Black's Law Dict. 6th Ed., Page 1083).

DUPLICATE GOVERNMENTS, DUPLICATE COURTS, AND, DUPLICATE CITIZENS

OUR TWO U.S. GOVERNMENTS

Under the American Constitution, there is the **"National Government of the _(united)_ States", representing our Union of States, a Republic;** and there is the <u>lesser</u> _"federal" foreign affairs and military jurisdiction_ under Article 1, Section 8 of our same Constitution. _In the lesser federal jurisdiction_ our President acts as "Commander-In-Chief" to maintain control of the nation, which has with banker influence _(manipulation with money)_, presently manipulated itself into power calling itself a _"democracy"_, though diluted and not true in reality. <u>It only possesses fiction _"citizens"_ without birth rights</u>! This switch of national power and constitutional manipulation, called a _"coup d'é·tat"_ was executed and achieved gradually over at least five to six decades by our liberal, unpatriotic, compromising elected officials and political, banker influenced, <u>socialist minded judges who are appointed by weak, Godless, liberal-minded, socialist bent Presidents</u>. These determinedly deny we _"Nationals"_ our sovereign State birth rights

47

(inalienable rights) as American *"Private Citizens"* in order to sustain a pretentious, corrupt banker controlled, diluted democracy of misinformed fiction *"citizens"*.

The President is today <u>elected only</u> by second-class, knowledge starved, ignorant U.S. federal fiction *"<u>c</u>itizens"*, not by sovereign American National Private Citizens, who are denied their lawful right to vote *(<u>**disfranchised**</u>[19] unless they change and subordinate their citizenship to that of the <u>lesser</u> federal jurisdiction)*.

THE PRESIDENCY (TWO OFFICES)

The "Presidency" of the Republic consists of two Offices. One is called the *"President"*, the *National Office*. This Office presides with the <u>National Congress of the Republic</u> and its Government which is missing in action *(at present, he's presently imitating that Office)*.

The President's other, <u>lesser Office</u> *(federal)*, is that of the acting senior military commander, or *"Commander-In-Chief"*. This Office presides over the military and federal jurisdiction, and

---

19 Disfranchise. To deprive of the rights and privileges of a free citizen; to deprive of chartered rights and immunities; to deprive of any franchise, as of the right of voting in elections, etc... (Source: Black's Law Dict. 6th Ed. Page 468.

in times of national emergency, can function over the nation as such. He presently exercises his Presidential authority as "Commander-In-Chief" by using military *"Executive Orders"*[20] at will. The federal *"Executive Order"* is an order or regulation issued by the President *(almost exclusively - while acting as the Commander-In-Chief)* or by some administrative authority under his direction for the purpose of interpreting, implementing, or giving administrative effect to a provision of the Constitution or of some law or treaty.

To have the effect of law, such orders must be published in the *"Federal Register"* (See *"Federal Register"* in Footnote 31).

(Author's Note: The Executive Order was never initiated to legislate or make (create) law in peacetime, which is a present inappropriate and abusive application!)

OUR TWO SUPREME COURTS
OUR *"ONE SUPREME COURT"*:

---

20 **Executive order.** (Source: Black's Law Dict. 6th Ed., Page 569) Author's Note: The First Executive Order was issued by Abraham Lincoln during the Civil War (exigency = urgency; emergency etc.) because he did not have a quorum in Congress with which to pass favorable law. Now used with regularity, regardless of emergency or military need.

There are also two Supreme Courts, the *"**One Supreme Court**"* under the ***American National Constitution of the Republic*** *(An Article III Court - PRESENTLY VACANT)* which is the lawful, competent, rightful and proper Supreme Court for the *American People and the Republic.* This is the rightful court jurisdiction of the 48 Star Flag of our Union of States, a Republic.

THEIR FEDERAL U.S. SUPREME COURT

Within this very same Constitution there also exists the <u>lesser</u> Article I jurisdiction ***Federal United States Supreme Court,*** which unfortunately is <u>now impersonating</u> the *"**One Supreme Court**"* of the American Republic and our Union of States.

JURISDICTIONAL COURT FLAGS

The ***Positive law, American Flag of the Republic*** of **48 Stars** does not fly in their Godless federal courtrooms, only the 50 star federal jurisdiction military flag does. Additionally, the present federal jurisdiction Article 1 Courts, agencies etc. will, <u>without your permission</u> and exceeding their lawful authority, convert your proper birth name on legal documents to the ALL CAPITALIZED printed fiction name. This corruption of justice is done in order bring you under their foreign federal jurisdiction 50 star flag Article 1 courts of legislated laws as a lesser in right *"public citizen"* of Washington D.C.

OUR TWO TYPES OF CITIZENS

OUR STATE'S BORN AMERICAN NATIONAL, A SOVEREIGN

The living soul *(e.g. American National Private Citizen, a State's born sovereign of the Republic)* is a "freeman" with inalienable State's birthrights and his birth name *(seal)* intact.

THE FICTION, CREATED FEDERAL *"EMANCIPATED SLAVE"* CITIZEN

There is also the Federal Government created impersonator of that living soul *(a legal fiction)*, titled the U.S. *"public citizen"* or *"citizen"*, who by contract has become burdened and bound with debt *(income taxes)*. The confirmation of the abusive federal *(military jurisdiction)* being in control is the simple fact that American State's born sovereign *Private Citizens* in their lawful birth names are dishonored by the Federal Government in all respects and cannot even vote unless they subjugate their birth names and inalienable birth rights. <u>They are *disfranchised* at the polls</u>!

I was always taught that the devil was a liar and deceiver... when our lying politicians, judges, attorneys, civil servants and bankers do the same, it should make you wonder who they work for (?)

Beware of the Pharisees!

KNOW YOUR HISTORY
AND YOUR RIGHTS

Learn about our proper government and learn how to lawfully protect yourself and your rights! Your inalienable Private Citizen birth rights, freedoms and liberties are at stake! This is your responsibility in order that you and your children can be protected from greater government abuse, bondage and tyrannical actions by empowered, unethical people using deceptive government civil service practices. Learn the truth about your citizenship and birthrights and then properly and lawfully reclaim them if you are functioning as a federal U.S. *"public citizen"* under a *"legal fiction"* name. If you check your Driver's License, Social Security Card, Credit Cards, and Birth Certificate and find that you are foreign to the *American Constitution of the Republic* and as an American born, also foreign to your State's rights *(common-law of your birth State)* you have no *"inalienable"* birth rights. Surprised? You should be.

***Freedom is not free! That
right is secured at a price.***

What price are you willing to pay?

"Good men, without knowledge of their
government that provides them freedom,
shall soon loose their freedom and liberty
only to be enslaved, because of indifference
and ignorance."

- Author

THE PRIVATE CITIZEN'S REWARD FOR SUBMISSION TO THE FEDERAL JURISDICTION IS LOSS OF RIGHTS, DEGENERATION AND BONDAGE.

OUR EDUCATORS, OUR JURISTS AND OUR CIVIL SERVANTS:

Today, liberal, federalized public educators in our school systems profit most from federal and state assistance grants *(hush-money or "buy-off" money)*. They teach and do what the feds tell them to teach and practice, and they will not bite the hand that feeds them. I fault our liberal educators for the "Dumbing" down of our children of America. I also find that our corrupted judicial systems consisting of inept administrators, corrupt attorneys and sold out, un-American judges, being Godless, are far removed from the reality of our proper State and American Constitutions and the American People they are supposed to serve with honor and integrity. All these, as groupings appear to have sold their souls, compromised their values and the values of our great country for temporal gain of personal prestige, position and social prestige of community and *"federal debt note"* paper money. These have blindly either compromised, abandoned, or maybe even sold their integrity, *(assuming that they had some in the first place)* and the positive evidences today are the corrupted values of several generations of young children and adults... all because they refuse to teach and honor God and His Truth. They refuse to look at us, the *American National,* and *sovereign,* as the great economic power and foundational source of their personal gain. Instead, these weak minded, dependent educators and civil servants are repeatedly chummed with enticements and look to the irresponsible, banker controlled, U.S. Federal Government for handouts ($$$$$) to pay and maintain themselves in their subservient, compromising, carnal and limited ways. They allow themselves to be in constant federal bondage to misguided philosophies, estranged truths and outright deceptions for financial security and gain. This same type of thinking has permeated our politicians and civil servants to where they think that because they control the money they can now rule and control us with debt *(federal notes = fiat money)* paper dollars instead of us ruling and controlling them. Our elected officials and civil servants from Washington D.C. to the lowest level of our communities have become self-serving, fearless and arrogant.

CITIZENSHIP IS VOLUNTARY

"Those people who are not governed by
God will be ruled by Tyrants."

-William Penn

TESTING OF BIRTH NAME
AND BIRTH RIGHTS IN
COURTS OF LAW

The properly spelled birth right name versus the printed ALL CAPITALIZED legal fiction name has been affirmed as to the distinguishing of jurisdiction, at law, in the following *United States Court for the Hawaii District*[21] cases:

96-01177; 97-00239; 97-01050; 98-00089; 98-00252; 98-00418; 98-00574; 00-00048; Also, Los Angeles Superior Court – Central District, Case No. BS-052162 (Sept. 2, 1998)

It has also been tested in dozens of de facto *(unlawful, but in power)* Puppet STATE OF HAWAII District Court cases. These herein stated facts of truth have never been refuted nor proven wrong in any of the filed and documented cases of record. The fact is that judges within both *(federal)* state and U.S. Federal Courts, in full collusive participation with Attorneys *(Members of the Bar Association)* openly acting in violation of law, capture jurisdiction

---

21 **U.S. Court for the Hawaii District.** The supposedly lawful court's jurisdiction does not include the Islands of the Hawaiian Archipelago (affirmed in 28 USC 91) and its judges are under modified, fraudulent oaths of Office that are not in compliance with Title 28 USC 453.

of the *"National"*, a living soul *(natural man)* by unlawfully converting the properly spelled, English language birth name to the improper *"legal fiction"* name in their court filings. This outrageous ignoring and abuse of American rights to justice, private rights, and truth, is done as if these legalists are under a great devious and demonic secret oath, greater than that lawfully required under **28 U.S. C. § 453** to honor Almighty God and Country.

UNGODLY OATHS OF OFFICE

We assume all justices and attorneys have supposedly taken oath to honor Almighty God and Country for our People; our Constitution, Treaties *(Supreme law)*; and laws *(to protect all types of citizens)*. **Yet, as legalists, they have not and they do not!** *(NOTE: In the de facto Puppet STATE OF HAWAII judiciary, there is no commitment or oath to honor Almighty God. How about the judges in your State?)*. Therefore, attorneys sworn in by these *"bastard oath"* judges are also of questionable commitment to righteousness.

Justice has been prostituted! A questionable, Godless *(not knowing right from wrong)*, judicial system, including attorneys, has deliberately, with knowledge of truth, permitted the concealment and theft of our birthrights! They have diminished and squelched our freedoms and liberties! Today, these judges and attorneys believe their law is god and they are greater than Almighty God! They do not know my God or His ways and most definitely do not call on Him or His Word for guidance. They are fools!

The Lord God says in *Isaiah, Chapter 59,* *"...justice is turned away backward, and righteousness stands afar off; for truth has fallen in to the street (gutter) and equity cannot enter."* Today, this is a truthful statement.

JUDICIAL CORRUPTION

The American judicial system is a failure. It has unfortunately become the sole justice system of very politically liberal, socialistic, unjust, and corrupted, "federalized" judges. They are oblivious to our State and National Constitutions of the Republic and our American *"Private Citizen"* sovereign State's rights. Lacking integrity, they no longer carry the respect, honor and dignity that the American Constitution and we free American *National*

Citizens require of our justice systems.

OUR PRIVATE CITIZENSHIP FAILURE

The massive political corruption of our judicial systems and government is also caused by our own personal failure as a free American People to seek awareness, knowledge, understanding, and respect for our American birth rights and to maintain authority and control over the actions of politicians and our appointed judges. We have allowed judges without Godly or even good moral values *(who are liars, manipulators and abusers of the law)*. to sit in judgment over us.

We have refused to stand up and fight for our freedoms and citizenship rights to protect our children and our children's children.

We are all failures: We have not stood up for the *"**righteousness**"*[22] of Almighty God!

---

22 Righteous. 1. characterized by uprightness or morality: a righteous observance of the law. 2. morally right or justifiable: righteous indignation. 3. acting in an upright, moral way; virtuous: a righteous and godly person... (Source: Webster's Encyclopedic Unabridged Dictionary, 2001 Ed.) AUTHOR'S NOTE: The words "righteous" and "righteousness" DO NOT APPEAR in Black's Law Dictionary. That should tell us something about or legal system.

CHANGING OF BABIES BIRTH NAMES ON BIRTH CERTIFICATES

The corporate city, state and federal jurisdictions, <u>without conscience</u>, change the names of babies and minors *(unlawfully)* without consent, to the printed ALL CAPITALIZED *"legal fiction"* names without the explicit consent, knowledge and awareness of the parents, for a reason. This action under law, previously mentioned, is called *"constructive fraud"* because it's premeditated on false and misleading pretenses to gain an advantage over the child. The parents of this post-war generation of children *(since World War II)* have been kept ignorant *(e.g. not taught the truth by our paid liberal and blind educators in grammar schools, high schools and colleges about their inalienable and fundamental rights and the power and freedom possessed in their lawful birth names).* These precious children, ill taught and lacking knowledge, are in life easily misled by others to be bound by contracts that take away and keep away their rights.

UNLAWFUL NAME CHANGERS

Our public servants think they have become

our masters. This is why judges, politicians, civil servants, and hospital staff, without fear of retribution, change the names of babies on birth certificates prior to registering them in the Department of Health *(Commerce)* of your City, County or State. <u>The hospitals even coerce new parents to register the child for a social security number as if a primary obligation of the hospital. The hospital assumes a misrepresentation liability for failure to divulge the truth *(facts)* when it does so.</u> These hospitals assist in making the living soul *(baby)* a property or *"thing"* of the State, and function as subordinate federal jurisdictions. When the parents who have the legal and lawful right to stop the procedure do not, but condone it by ignorance, they have in fact given *(permitted legal adoption, acquiesced, submitted)* their babies to the State i.e. federal jurisdiction. Yet, the parents still have the responsibility to raise that child within the legal State *(as the State dictates)*, after having signed away God's righteousness and inalienable birth rights.

SILENT, ACTIVE IDENTITY THEFT

In the de facto Puppet STATE OF HAWAII *(and possibly in your state)*, <u>and in our hospitals,</u>

the lawful and proper English language spelled names of babies are unlawfully changed to fictions by these federalized agencies of the de facto state and cooperating Department of Health *(Commerce)*. Functioning in commerce, the Department of Health changes the names *(federalizes [or monetizes] the Birth Certificate to create a mortgage document)* to create ALL CAPITALIZED *"legal fictions"* in violation of law and right and without the parents explicit understanding and lawful knowledge of the consequences of such change. <u>This is outright corruption, identity theft and fraud by the federalized de facto Puppet State</u>! This fact is easily confirmed. The only reason for doing so is to make the innocent child a *"bond servant"* and *"ward of the State"* *(legally, but not lawfully adopted)* ignoring lawful birthrights and authority of the parents. In America, it removes one from under most of the *American Constitution* and places the child under *Article 1, Section 8 (the federal jurisdiction)* of that same Constitution.

In Hawaii, it removes the child from the de jure ***"Hawaiian Kingdom National Constitution"***, their foreign birth rights and National *"common-law"*… and makes them *(foreign)*, second-class 14th Amendment

United States *"public citizens"* of the U.S. Federal jurisdiction <u>while they are domiciled on their own Hawaiian National birth soil</u>. This massive pre-programmed U.S. Federal Government corruption is executed through our ignorance, to take away our rights and freedoms!

CONTRACTS THAT CHANGE LIVES

Fact: Contracts entered into, <u>with the fullness of knowledge</u>, are binding upon those who enter into them, <u>unless fraud is evident</u> as in theft of our names for the sake of removing us from our birth rights, which provide us our inalienable rights.

The <u>corporate federalized states</u> *(not sovereign States)* that function under Article 1 Section 8 comply by converting your birth name through a Birth Certificate, Driver's License or State Identification Card. These are designed to get you to be identified as a federal *"person"*, *"citizen" or "corporate entity"*. They, <u>without your knowledge</u>, encourage you to sign away your birth rights *(inalienable rights)* and birth name in order to move you to their <u>lesser</u> jurisdiction and its taxable bondage within their federal family *(enclave)*.

The U.S. Federal Government also captures you through federal contracts *(remember the law of the flag?)*... primarily an implied federal *"**adhesion contract**"*[23] called the *Social Security Act*, affirmed by your signature *(seal)* and your acceptance of their Social Security Identification Number and Card. Another way is for them to intimidate and demand that you obtain a "Employer's Excise Number" or Tax I.D. Number or form a corporation *(even a non-profit)* wherein you as an officer, in their jurisdiction, are financially liable for the total debt *(even if you are only a kind helper to make the corporation a corporation by volunteering your services)*.

Today, as mentioned, our hospitals will entice the parents of a newborn child to register the infant for a Social Security Number. The solicitor, usually a staff nurse or administrator, is partaking in an unlawful

---

23 Adhesion contract. Standardized contract form offered to consumers of goods and services on essentially "take it or leave it" basis without affording consumer realistic opportunity to bargain and under such conditions that consumer cannot obtain desired product or services except by acquiescing in form contract. Distinctive feature of adhesion contract is that weaker party has no realistic choice as to its terms.... Recognizing that these contracts are not the result of traditionally "bargained" contracts, the trend is to relieve parties from onerous conditions imposed by such contracts. However, not every such contract is unconscionable... (Source: Black's Law Dict. 6th Ed., Page 40)

act of misrepresenting not just the nature of
the Social Security Act, but failing to notify
the parents that the parents have no lawful
authority to sign away their minor child's birth
rights to a foreign jurisdiction of government
or agency that the hospital, <u>without a lawful
license to do so</u>, represents. It is time for
young parents to put these federal agents
who work in hospitals to the test of law for
misrepresentation and fraud. I would love
to see the hospital's license or authority to
make such misrepresentations to stressed,
vulnerable, new parents who have not been
properly informed of their own lawful rights.

THERE'S EVEN PASSPORT FRAUD

Unfortunately, even our **U.S. Passport**
names are unlawfully converted by the federal
jurisdiction to a created fiction name without
our explicit authorization and to violate our
inalienable, lawful birth rights. This falsely
portrays to the world that we are a bound,
enslaved *"public citizen"* or *"corporate entity"*
of the federal jurisdiction and not free born as
"American National" "Private Citizens". This
is most definitely, more federal government
corruption!

SELLING YOUR CHILD'S BIRTH CERTIFICATE FOR FINANCIAL GAIN

Your <u>corporate federalized state</u> takes your original birth certificate, places a monetary border around it, and creates a banker's ***"Bearer Bond"***[24] and ***"Bearer Instrument"***[25] which is also a ***"Bearer Document"***[26] mortgaging you or your children under your fiction name to the U.S Federal Treasury *(e.g. **"Federal Reserve"**[27])* as a <u>debtor</u>. My belief is that this maneuver also transfers your now modified birth certificate to Washington, D.C. *(U.S. Treasury)* to convert you to a debtor *"**c**itizen"* of Washington, D.C., <u>at least on paper</u>. You

---

24 Bearer Bond. Bonds payable to the person having possession of them. Such bonds do not require endorsement to transfer ownership but only the transfer of possession. (Source: Black's Law Dict. 6th Ed. Page 154)

25 Bearer instrument. An instrument is payable to bearer when by its terms it is payable to (a) bearer or the order of bearer; or (b) a specified person or bearer; or (c) "cash" or the order of "cash", or any other indication which does not purport to designate a specific payee. U.C.C. §§ 3-111, 3-204(2). (Source: Black's Law Dict. 6th Ed. Page 154)

26 Bearer document. A document that runs to bearer upon issuance or after a blank endorsement, and that is negotiated by delivery alone. U.C.C. §§ 7-501(1) & (2)(a), Anyone in possession of a bearer document is a holder of it. U.C.C § 1-201(20) (Source: Black's Law Dict. 6th Ed., Page 154)

27 Federal Reserve. (Author's Note) The Federal Reserve is a private pure trust of bankers, et al, given authority and power to run and control the American monetary system under the U.S. Treasury by then President Franklin D. Roosevelt through the Federal Reserve Act of 1933.

are now a <u>mortgaged</u>, U.S. Federal *"citizen"*, *"person"* or *"thing"* outside of the *American Constitution of the Republic*, <u>without birth rights</u> and burdened with substantial tax debt e.g. as a ***"bond servant"***[28].

<u>This evil, corrupt act is then enforced by the liberal, socialistic minded, political judges within the Article I court federalized jurisdictions.</u> This conversion under government law, as I have previously mentioned, is called *"constructive fraud"* of the highest corrupt, criminal order; because those bankers, politicians and judges in present power *(who partake and enforce)* do it with the fullness of knowledge and with the deliberate intent to deceive; a premeditated grand plan and scheme with criminal intent.

HOW IT WORKS

Here's the deal. As I see it, if on a document you use their fictitious name that they own, and upon which you ignorantly placed your guarantee *(your "Seal" = "Signature")* to honor that document, you have contracted. Now, the U.S. Federal Treasury *(e.g.*

---

28 Bond servant. 1. a person who serves in bondage; slave. 2. a person bound to service without wages. (Source: Webster's Encyclopedic Dict. 2001 Ed.) Author's Note: Not found in Black's Law Dictionary.

intimidated by and submitting its power to, the Federal Reserve) can assess / place a debt upon that fiction name that you are using, let's say, $500,000.00 to more than $1,000,000.00. Now you in your lifetime must pay tribute to the *"federal money god"* *(e.g. known as the private, pure trust, Federal Reserve to whom the Federal U.S. is greatly and irresponsibly indebted - i.e. to bankers).* You owe the assessed income taxes *(lien)* for the privilege of using their name. You have now with your signatured consent, transferred yourself into their federal jurisdiction. You, without question, are using their name which you acknowledged with your signature (seal)... getting the picture? With your birth certificate modified and pledged by your city, county and federalized state as security, you have willingly become a paper Federal U.S. *"public citizen"* or *"bond servant"* of Washington D.C., a federal enclave.

We have failed! We, the American People, have not stood up for the *"righteousness"*[29]

---

29 **Righteous.** 1. characterized by uprightness or morality: a righteous observance of the law. 2. morally right or justifiable: righteous indignation. 3. acting in an upright, moral way; virtuous: a righteous and godly person... (Source: Webster's Encyclopedic Unabridged Dictionary, 2001 Ed.) AUTHOR'S NOTE: The words "righteous" and "righteousness" DO NOT APPEAR in Black's Law Dictionary. That should tell us something about our legal system.

of **Almighty God! We need to get right with God, get involved and get control of our government again!**

CITIZENSHIP IS VOLUNTARY

CONCLUSION:

ABOUT IRS "INCOME TAXES" AND THE FICTION CITIZEN

The proof of the pudding is in the eating. Fact: If you are American born *(within one of the 48 States)* and <u>have cancelled your fraudulent, unlawful contract</u> and are <u>not</u> under the printed ALL CAPITALIZED *"legal fiction"* name and their foreign fifty star federal military flag, you do not owe and are not liable for federal U.S. ***"Income Taxes"***[30] any more than any other foreign nation's citizen.

If you read closely the Black's Law Dictionary definitions for those liable for *"Income Tax" (See Footnote 30)* you will find that <u>there is no *"income tax"* on *"Private Citizens"*</u>, that is, <u>State's born American Nationals, or sovereigns</u>. That liability only applies to U.S. Federal *"public citizens"*, e.g. *"Emancipated slaves" or "bond servants"* who hold the government office of *"Taxpayer"* in their

---

30 Income Tax. A tax on the yearly profits arising from property, professions, trades and offices. 2 Steph. Comm. 573 (Source: Black's Law Dict. 1st Ed. Page 611) "Income tax." A tax on the yearly profit arising from property, professions, trades, and offices. 2 Steph. Comm. 573. Levi v. Louisville, 97 Ky. 394, 30 S. W. 973, 28 L. R. A. 480; Parker v. Insurance Co., 42 La. Ann. 428 7 South. 599. (Source: Black's Law Dict. 2nd Ed. Page 612) NOT FOUND IN THE 6TH EDITION OF BLACK'S LAW DICTIONARY, WONDER WHY?

Washington D.C. jurisdiction.

THE IRS "NONRESIDENT ALIEN"

The *American National Private Citizen, or sovereign,* within the United States Code Title 26 is called a ***"nonresident alien"***. This is because they are not *"residents" (domiciled)* within a federal or military jurisdiction and they are *"alien"* to it *(they have not been jurisdictionally converted);* nor do they reside in one of the five federal IRS *"States"* defined therein as, Washington D.C., Guam, Puerto Rico, American Samoa or American Virgin Islands; nor derive their income directly from the Federal United States; nor are they corporate *"officers"*.

Section 871(a) of Title 26, states that *"nonresident aliens"* are subject to: " **...a tax of 30 percent of the amount received from sources within the United States by a nonresident alien individual as -... (etc.)"** *(This applies <u>only to income from within</u> the U.S. Federal jurisdiction -Author).* That would be a shocking tax, except that if you read Title 26 closely, <u>you will find that Section 871 is to be ignored as earlier stated</u> *(in Section 32.)* under "Earned Income.", where under 32(c)

(2)(B)(iii) it states: **"no amount to which section 871 (a) applies (relating to income of nonresident alien individuals not connected with United States business) shall be taken into account..."** Under Section 32(c)(E) a *"nonresident alien"* is not to be included as one liable *(for income taxes)* unless he or she *"elects" (or volunteers)* to contribute *(e.g. "...by reason of election...").*

The Internal Revenue Code (IRS) is not "Positive law" by their own IRS admission in their IRS statement made in **Title 26 of the United States Code, Section 7806 (a) and (b).**

Please read: I now quote Section 7806:

"Construction of Title (Title 26, IRS Code) (a) The cross references in this title to other portions of the title, or other provisions of law, where the word "see" is used, are made only for convenience, and shall be given no legal effect. (b) No inference, implication, or presumption of legislative construction shall be drawn or made by reason of the location or grouping of any particular section or provision or portion of this title, nor shall any table of contents, table of cross references, or similar outline, analysis, or descriptive matter

relating to the contents of this title be given any legal effect. The preceding sentence also applies to the side notes and ancillary tables contained in the various prints of this Act before its enactment into law."

I repeat, the IRS Code has never been "... *enacted into law"* (e.g. read into the *"Federal Register"*[31] *to become binding* Positive law for American National Private Citizens).

American National Private Citizens are bound by righteousness and obligated to honor *Positive law*, not this demonic, banker created, federal statutory impersonation of law. *The Internal Revenue Code (IRS) (the collection agency for the Federal Reserve)* is therefore only suggestion to *American Nationals (nonresident aliens)*! The IRS Code really only applies to created U.S. Federal *"public citizens"* or *"persons"* within that specific

---

31 Federal Register. The Federal Register, published daily, is the medium for making available to the public Federal agency regulations and other legal documents of the executive branch. These documents cover a wide range of Government activities. An important function of the Federal Register is that it includes proposed changes (rules, regulations, standards, etc.) of governmental agencies. Each proposed change published carries an invitation for any citizen or group to participate in the consideration of the proposed regulation through the submission of written data, views, or arguments, and sometimes oral presentations. Such regulations and rules as finally approved appear thereafter in the Code of Federal Regulations. (Source: Black's Law Dict. 6th Ed., Page 612.)

jurisdiction. So why honor it? Intimidated? Is it fear? **Fear is not from God!** Whom do you trust? Why would you want to be a <u>lesser</u>, *"federal <u>c</u>itizen"* without birth rights and inalienable rights?

Remember: You who are American Nationals... **the 16th Amendment *(for a <u>national</u> income tax)* was never lawfully ratified *(approved)* by the independent, sovereign States of the Union! <u>American Nationals are still not lawfully taxed!</u> Today, only those who identify themselves as U.S. federal *"<u>c</u>itizens"* are taxed.**

My deduction, based upon actions of the Internal Revenue Service (IRS) and other agencies including the *U.S. Federal Courts* is that the printed ALL CAPITALIZED name denotes a *"person"* endued with *"Public Office"* as a ***"Public Official"***[32] (e.g. ***"Taxpayer"***[33]) within the federal jurisdiction. That being the case, it is my conclusion that this would be sufficient IRS justification for the IRS's lack of / or need for, proper, lawful service; and, further justify their abusive

---

32 Public Official. An officer; a person invested with the authority of an office. (Source: Black's Law Dict. 6th Ed. Page 1084.) Author's Note: The official office of "Taxpayer" would be appropriate for this justification.

use of unsigned liens, assuming that the U.S. Government Public Office held by you is that of a *"Taxpayer"*[33]. **The IRS adjudicates against you based upon <u>your violation</u> of the federal *"implied contract"*, not their violation.**

The Cure: The best way to defeat a sickness or cancer is to eat properly to provide the anti-bodies that kill the cancer cells. Similarly, the best way to defeat a corrupt, evil and demonic element in our society is to expose it to the light *(God's Truth)* which will kill it.

TRUTH REVEALS AND DESTROYS EVIL!

---

33 Taxpayer. A person whose income is subject to taxation; one from whom government demands a pecuniary contribution towards its support. (Black's Law Dict. 6th Ed., Page 1459) (Author's Note: "Person" in this sense would be a federal, created entity, or "citizen".)

ENOUGH ABOUT THE IRS
AND INCOME TAXES

There is much to learn about your birth name and birth rights which establishes and preserves your freedoms. It all starts with how you spell your name and what you accept by contract and become obligated for. Read the 14th Amendment and understand that this was at the end of the Civil War (1868). Note: You may have noticed in this text the use of the small, underlined, lower case *"c"* for *"citizen" (identifying the federal "citizen*. The Constitutional Amendments prior to the 14th Amendment used the capital "C" to denote the *"Private Citizen"*, a State's born sovereign. After the 14th Amendment the lower case "c" is used for the federal *"citizen"*, e.g. the government created, *"Emancipated Slave"*.

There is a great and powerful distinction between inalienable rights possessed by the State's rights birthed *"American National Private Citizen"* or sovereign, versus the non-rights and licensing required of this fictitious government created, subordinate, federal *"public citizen"*. **The *"Private Citizen"* is a *free* man** while the other is still a *"bond servant"* *(Emancipated Slave),* but now under federal

<u>license and being given a benefit</u>. If you are using the printed ALL CAPITALIZED name out of ignorance and want to restore your American National Private Citizen State's birth rights, you must sever the contract properly. Fellow Americans... there is a right and lawfully proper way to do all things. **Remember, your birth rights are preserved and retained in your proper, English language spelled birth name! Get them back!**

NOTE: Godless attorneys and judges within these legal systems will tell you: *"Ignorance of the law is no excuse!"* Yet these are the same who hide TRUTH and the knowledge of law and perpetuate federal fraud upon us through their devious, misguided and deliberate actions. **<u>Wake up America</u>! We are being destroying as a free and caring People, by those abusing law!**

The choice is still yours. You can live anywhere in this world you want. The only thing you must do is honor that particular countries law and their people's rights, customs and traditions, and that fact pertains <u>even to America</u>! Our attorneys, judges and politicians have proven themselves to be un-American and not trustworthy. They focus primarily on the dollar, the bankers who create it, and the influential; while ignoring our needs and the righteousness of Almighty God. It is time for major positive, constructive political change in America.

The American National Citizens must re-claim their birth rights; and their American National Republic and its Union of States!

My Prayer: May our Private Citizens, American Union of States and our Republic be restored and preserved in dignity, "Under Almighty God".

AMERICAN, I LOVE YOU!

Citizenship is voluntary and your God Given inalienable birth rights are preserved in your State's birth, properly spelled birth name!

Jesus Christ is still on the Throne of God and it is in His Righteousness that we must act.

IT IS TIME FOR AMERICANS
TO SAVE THEIR OWN COUNTRY!

Dated: March 21, 2009

Respectfully,

Aran Alton: Ardaiz,
American National and
Private Citizen

FOR ADDITIONAL INFORMATION:

Contact:
The Truth of God Ministry
Email: *TruthofGodMinistry@Hawaii.rr.com*

Other books by Aran Alton Ardaiz:

HAWAII: The Fake State

HAWAIIAN BIRTHRIGHTS:
Understanding "Hawaiian National" Private
Citizen Birth Rights

"Woe to those judges who issue unrighteous decrees, and to the magistrates who keep causing unjust and oppressive decisions to be recorded, to turn aside the needy from justice and to make plunder of the rightful claim of the poor of My people, that widows may be their spoil, and that they may make the fatherless their prey!

(Holy Bible, Isaiah 10: 1, 2

Printed in the United States
149442LV00002B/3/P

9 780615 297347